PROTOCOL
AMENDING THE CONVENTION
BETWEEN
THE GOVERNMENT OF THE UNITED STATES OF AMERICA
AND
THE GOVERNMENT OF THE FRENCH REPUBLIC
FOR THE AVOIDANCE OF DOUBLE TAXATION
AND THE PREVENTION OF FISCAL EVASION
WITH RESPECT TO TAXES ON INCOME AND CAPITAL,
SIGNED AT PARIS ON AUGUST 31, 1994,
AS AMENDED BY THE PROTOCOL SIGNED ON DECEMBER 8, 2004

THE GOVERNMENT OF THE UNITED STATES OF AMERICA

AND

THE GOVERNMENT OF THE FRENCH REPUBLIC

DESIRING to amend the Convention Between the Government of the United States of America and the Government of the French Republic for the Avoidance of Double Taxation and the Prevention of Fiscal Evasion with Respect to Taxes on Income and Capital, signed at Paris on August 31, 1994, as amended by the Protocol signed at Washington on December 8, 2004 ("the Convention"), have agreed as follows:

ARTICLE I

1. Subparagraph b) (iii) of paragraph 2 of Article 4 (Resident) of the Convention shall be deleted and replaced by the following:

> "(iii) in the case of the United States, a regulated investment company, a real estate investment trust, and a real estate mortgage investment conduit; in the case of France, a "société d'investissement à capital variable" (SICAV), a "société d'investissement immobilier cotée" (SIIC), a "société de placement à prépondérance immobilière à capital variable" (SPPICAV); and any similar investment entities agreed upon by the competent authorities of both Contracting States."

2. Subparagraphs b) (iv), (b) (v), and (b) (vi) of paragraph 2 of Article 4 (Resident) of the Convention shall be deleted.

3. New subparagraph c) of paragraph 2 of Article 4 (Resident) of the Convention shall be added as follows:

"c) An item of income paid from the United States to a French qualified partnership shall be considered derived by a resident of France only to the extent that such income is included currently in the taxable income of a shareholder, associate or other member that is otherwise treated as a resident of France under the provisions of this Convention. A French qualified partnership means a partnership:

(i) that has its place of effective management in France,

(ii) that has not elected to be taxed in France as a corporation,

(iii) the tax base of which is computed at the partnership level for French tax purposes, and

(iv) all of the shareholders, associates or other members of which, pursuant to the tax laws of France, are liable to tax therein in respect of their share of the profits of that partnership."

4. New paragraph 3 of Article 4 (Resident) of the Convention shall be added as follows:

"3. For purposes of applying this Convention, an item of income, profit or gain derived through an entity that is fiscally transparent under the laws of either Contracting State, and that is formed or organized:

a) in either Contracting State, or;

b) in a state that has concluded an agreement containing a provision for the exchange of information with a view to the prevention of tax evasion with the Contracting State from which the income, profit, or gain is derived,

shall be considered to be derived by a resident of a Contracting State to the extent that the item is treated for purposes of the taxation law of such Contracting State as the income, profit or gain of a resident."

5. Paragraphs 3 and 4 of Article 4 (Resident) of the Convention shall be renumbered as paragraphs 4 and 5.

ARTICLE II

Article 10 (Dividends) of the Convention shall be deleted and replaced by the following:

"Article 10

Dividends

1. Dividends paid by a company that is a resident of a Contracting State to a resident of the other Contracting State may be taxed in that other State.

2. However, such dividends may also be taxed in the Contracting State of which the company paying the dividends is a resident and according to the laws of that State, but if the beneficial owner of the dividends is a resident of the other Contracting State, the tax so charged shall not exceed:

a) 5 percent of the gross amount of the dividends if the beneficial owner is a company that owns:

(i) directly at least 10 percent of the voting stock of the company paying the dividends, if such company is a resident of the United States; or

(ii) directly or indirectly at least 10 percent of the capital of the company paying the dividends, if such company is a resident of France;

b) 15 percent of the gross amount of the dividends in all other cases.

3. Notwithstanding the provisions of paragraph 2, such dividends shall not be taxed in the Contracting State of which the company paying the dividends is a resident if the beneficial owner is a company that is a resident of the other Contracting State that has owned, directly or indirectly through one or more residents of either Contracting State, shares representing 80 percent or more of the voting power of the company paying the dividends in the case of the United States, or 80 percent or more of the capital of the company paying the dividends in the case of France, for a 12-month period ending on the date on which entitlement to the dividends is determined and:

a) satisfies the conditions of clause (i) or (ii) of subparagraph c) of paragraph 2 of Article 30 (Limitation on Benefits of the Convention);

b) satisfies the conditions of clauses (i) and (ii) of subparagraph e) of paragraph 2 of Article 30, provided that the company satisfies the conditions described in paragraph 4 of that Article with respect to the dividends;

c) is entitled to benefits with respect to the dividends under paragraph 3 of Article 30; or

d) has received a determination pursuant to paragraph 6 of Article 30 with respect to this paragraph.

4. Paragraphs 2 and 3 shall not affect the taxation of the company in respect of the profits out of which the dividends are paid.

5. a) Subparagraph a) of paragraph 2 and paragraph 3 shall not apply in the case of dividends paid by a U.S. Regulated Investment Company (RIC), a U.S. Real Estate Investment Trust (REIT), a French "société d'investissement à capital variable" (SICAV), a French "société d'investissement immobilier cotée" (SIIC), or a French "société de placement à prépondérance immobilière à capital variable" (SPPICAV).

b) In the case of dividends paid by a RIC or a SICAV, subparagraph (b) of paragraph 2 shall apply. In the case of dividends paid by a REIT, a SIIC or a SPPICAV, subparagraph (b) of paragraph 2 shall apply only if:

(i) the beneficial owner of the dividends is an individual, or a pension trust or other organization maintained exclusively to administer or provide retirement or employee benefits that is established or sponsored by a resident, in either case holding an interest of not more than 10 percent in the REIT, SIIC or SPPICAV;

(ii) the dividends are paid with respect to a class of shares that is publicly traded and the beneficial owner of the dividends is a person holding an interest of not more than 5 percent of any class of the REIT's, SIIC's or SPPICAV's shares; or

(iii) the beneficial owner of the dividends is a person holding an interest of not more than 10 percent in the REIT, SIIC or SPPICAV and, in the case of a REIT, such REIT is diversified.

c) For purposes of this paragraph, a REIT shall be "diversified" if the value of no single interest in real property exceeds 10 percent of its total interests in real property. For the purposes of this provision, foreclosure property shall not be considered an interest in real property. Where a REIT holds an interest in a partnership, it shall be treated as owning directly a proportion of the partnership's interests in real property corresponding to its interest in the partnership.

6. a) The term "dividends" means income from shares, "jouissance" shares or "jouissance" rights, mining shares, founders' shares or other rights, not being debt-claims, participating in profits, as well as income treated as a distribution by the taxation laws of the State of which the company making the distribution is a resident; and income from arrangements, including debt obligations, that carry the right to participate in, or are determined with reference to, profits of the issuer or one of its associated enterprises, as defined in subparagraph (a) or (b) of paragraph 1 of Article 9 (Associated Enterprises), to the extent that such income is characterized as a dividend under the law of the Contracting State in which the income arises. The term "dividend" shall not include income referred to in Article 16 (Directors' Fees).

b) The provisions of this Article shall apply where a beneficial owner of dividends holds depository receipts evidencing ownership of the shares in respect of which the dividends are paid, in lieu of the shares themselves.

7. The provisions of paragraphs 2 through 4 shall not apply if the beneficial owner of the dividends, being a resident of a Contracting State, carries on business in the other Contracting State, of which the company paying the dividends is a resident, through a permanent establishment situated therein, or performs in that other State independent personal services from a fixed base situated therein, and the dividends are attributable to such permanent establishment or fixed base. In such case, the provisions of Article 7 (Business Profits) or Article 14 (Independent Personal Services), as the case may be, shall apply.

8. a) A company that is a resident of a Contracting State and that has a permanent establishment in the other Contracting State, or that is subject to tax on a net basis in that other Contracting State on items of income that may be taxed in that other State under Article 6 (Income From Real Property) or under paragraph 1 of Article 13 (Capital Gains), may be subject in that other Contracting State to a tax in addition to the tax allowable under the other provisions of this Convention. Such tax, however, may be imposed only on the portion of the business profits of the company attributable to the permanent establishment and the portion of the income referred to in the preceding sentence that is subject to tax under Article 6 or paragraph 1 of Article 13 that,

> (i) in the case of the United States, represents the "dividend equivalent amount" of those profits and income; the term "dividend equivalent amount" shall, for the purposes of this subparagraph, have the meaning that it has under the law of the United States as it may be amended from time to time without changing the general principle thereof; and

> (ii) in the case of France, is included in the base of the French withholding tax in accordance with the provisions of Article 115 quinquies of the French tax code (Code général des impôts) or with any similar provisions which amend or replace the provisions of that Article.

b) The taxes referred to in subparagraph (a) also shall apply to the portion of the business profits, or of the income subject to tax under Article 6 (Income From Real Property) or paragraph 1 of Article 13 (Capital Gains) that is referred to in subparagraph (a), which is attributable to a trade or business conducted in one Contracting State through a partnership or other entity treated as a fiscally transparent entity under the laws of that State by a company that is a member of such partnership or entity and a resident of the other Contracting State.

9. The tax referred to in subparagraphs (a) and (b) of paragraph 8 shall not be imposed at a rate exceeding the rate specified in subparagraph (a) of paragraph 2. In any case, it shall not be imposed on a company that:

a) satisfies the conditions of clause (i) or (ii) of subparagraph (c) of paragraph 2 of Article 30 (Limitation on Benefits of the Convention);

b) satisfies the conditions of clauses (i) and (ii) of subparagraph (e) of paragraph 2 of Article 30, provided that the company satisfies the conditions described in paragraph 4 of that Article with respect to an item of income, profit, or gain described in paragraph 7;

c) is entitled under paragraph 3 of Article 30 to benefits with respect to an item of income, profit, or gain described in paragraph 7; or

d) has received a determination pursuant to paragraph 6 of Article 30 with respect to this paragraph.

10. Subject to the provisions of paragraph 8, where a company that is a resident of a Contracting State derives profits or income from the other Contracting State, that other State may not impose any tax on the dividends paid by the company, except insofar as such dividends are paid to a resident of that other State or insofar as the dividends are attributable to a permanent establishment or fixed base situated in that other State, nor subject the company's undistributed profits to a tax on the company's undistributed profits, even if the dividends paid or the undistributed profits consist wholly or partly of profits or income arising in such other State."

ARTICLE III

1. Paragraph 1 of Article 12 (Royalties) of the Convention shall be deleted and replaced by the following:

"1. Royalties arising in a Contracting State and beneficially owned by a resident of the other Contracting State shall be taxable only in that other State."

2. Paragraphs 2, 3, 4, and 5 of Article 12 (Royalties) of the Convention shall be deleted.

3. New paragraphs 2 and 3 of Article 12 (Royalties) of the Convention shall be added as follows:

"2. The term "royalties" as used in this Article means:

a) payments of any kind received as a consideration for the use of, or the right to use, any copyright of literary, artistic, or scientific work or any neighboring right (including reproduction rights and performing rights), any cinematographic film, any sound or picture recording, any software, any patent, trademark, design or model, plan, secret formula or process, or other like right or property, or for information concerning industrial, commercial, or scientific experience; and

b) gains derived from the alienation of any such right or property described in this paragraph that are contingent on the productivity, use, or further alienation thereof.

3. The provisions of paragraph 1 shall not apply if the beneficial owner of the royalties, being a resident of a Contracting State, carries on business in the other Contracting State, in which the royalties arise, through a permanent establishment situated therein, or performs in that State independent personal services from a fixed base situated therein, and the royalties are attributable to such permanent establishment or fixed base. In such case the provisions of Article 7 (Business Profits) or Article 14 (Independent Personal Services), as the case may be, shall apply."

4. Paragraphs 6 and 7 of Article 12 (Royalties) of the Convention shall be renumbered as paragraphs 4 and 5.

ARTICLE IV

Paragraph 5 of Article 13 (Capital Gains) of the Convention shall be deleted and replaced by the following:

"5. Gains described in subparagraph (b) of paragraph 2 of Article 12 (Royalties) shall be taxable only in accordance with the provisions of Article 12."

ARTICLE V

The last sentence of paragraph 1 of Article 17 (Artistes and Sportsmen) of the Convention shall be deleted and replaced by the following:

"However, the provisions of this paragraph shall not apply where the amount of the gross receipts derived by such entertainer or sportsman from such activities, including expenses reimbursed to him or borne on his behalf, does not exceed 10,000 United States dollars or its equivalent in euros for the taxable period concerned."

ARTICLE VI

The first sentence of paragraph 1 of Article 18 (Pensions) of the Convention shall be deleted and replaced by the following:

"Payments under the social security legislation or similar legislation of a Contracting State to a resident of the other Contracting State or to a citizen of the United States, and pension distributions and other similar remuneration arising in one of the Contracting States in consideration of past employment paid to a resident of the other Contracting State, whether paid periodically or in a lump sum, shall be taxable only in the first-mentioned State."

ARTICLE VII

Article 22 (Other Income) of the Convention shall be deleted and replaced by the following:

"Article 22

Other Income

1. Items of income beneficially owned by a resident of a Contracting State, wherever arising, not dealt with in the foregoing Articles of this Convention shall be taxable only in that State.

2. The provisions of paragraph 1 shall not apply to income, other than income from real property as defined in paragraph 2 of Article 6 (Income From Real Property), if the beneficial owner of such income, being a resident of a Contracting State, carries on business in the other Contracting State through a permanent establishment situated therein, or performs in that other State independent personal services from a fixed base situated therein, and the right or property in respect of which the income is paid is attributable to such permanent establishment or fixed base. In such case the provisions of Article 7 (Business Profits) or Article 14 (Independent Personal Services), as the case may be, shall apply."

ARTICLE VIII

1. Regarding Article 24 (Relief From Double Taxation) of the Convention as incorporated in the alternat of the United States, in both the English and French version of such alternat, paragraph 1 shall be renumbered paragraph 2, and paragraph 2 shall be renumbered paragraph 1.

2. Clause (iii) of subparagraph a) of paragraph 1 of Article 24 (Relief From Double Taxation) of the Convention, as amended by paragraph 1 of this Article VIII of this Protocol, shall be deleted and replaced by the following:

"(iii) in the case of income referred to in Article 10 (Dividends), Article 11 (Interest), paragraph 1 of Article 13 (Capital Gains), Article 16 (Director's Fees), and Article 17 (Artistes and Sportsmen), to the amount of tax paid in the United States in accordance with the provisions of the Convention; however, such credit shall not exceed the amount of French tax attributable to such income."

3. Clause (i) of subparagraph b) of paragraph 1 of Article 24 (Relief From Double Taxation) of the Convention, as amended by paragraph 1 of this Article VIII of this Protocol, shall be deleted and replaced by the following:

> "(i) income consisting of dividends paid by a company that is a resident of the United States, or interest arising in the United States, as described in paragraph 5 of Article 11 (Interest), or royalties arising in the United States, as described in paragraph 4 of Article 12 (Royalties), that is derived and beneficially owned by such individual and that is paid by:

>> aa) the United States or any political subdivision or local authority thereof; or

>> bb) a person created or organized under the laws of a state of the United States or the District of Columbia, the principal class of shares of or interests in which is substantially and regularly traded on a recognized stock exchange as defined in subparagraph (d) of paragraph 7 of Article 30 (Limitation on Benefits of the Convention); or

>> cc) a company that is a resident of the United States, provided that less than 10 percent of the outstanding shares of the voting power in such company was owned (directly or indirectly) by the resident of France at all times during the part of such company's taxable period preceding the date of payment of the income to the owner of the income and during the prior taxable period (if any) of such company, and provided that less than 50 percent of such voting power was owned (either directly or indirectly) by residents of France during the same period; or

>> dd) a resident of the United States, not more than 25 percent of the gross income of which for the prior taxable period (if any) consisted directly or indirectly of income derived from sources outside the United States;".

4. Clause (i) of subparagraph e) of paragraph 1 of Article 24 (Relief From Double Taxation) of the Convention as amended by paragraph 1 of this Article VIII of this Protocol, shall be deleted and replaced by the following:

> "(i) Where a company resident of France is taxed in that state according to French domestic law on a consolidated tax base, including the profits or losses of subsidiaries that are residents of the United States or of permanent establishments situated in the United States, the provisions of the Convention shall not prevent the application of that law."

5. Subparagraph (c) of paragraph 2 of Article 24 (Relief From Double Taxation) of the Convention, as amended by paragraph 1 of this Article VIII of this Protocol, shall be deleted.

ARTICLE IX

1. The last sentence of paragraph 2 of Article 25 (Non-Discrimination) shall be deleted and replaced by the following:

> "The provisions of this paragraph shall not prevent the application by either Contracting State of the taxes described in paragraph 8 of Article 10 (Dividends)."

2. The first sentence of clause a) of paragraph 3 of Article 25 shall be deleted and replaced by the following:

> "Except where the provisions of paragraph 1 of Article 9 (Associated Enterprises), paragraph 6 of Article 11 (Interest), or paragraph 5 of Article 12 (Royalties) apply, interest, royalties, and other disbursements paid by an enterprise of a Contracting State to a resident of the other Contracting State shall, for the purposes of determining the taxable profits of such enterprise, be deductible under the same conditions as if they had been paid to a resident of the first-mentioned State."

ARTICLE X

Paragraph 5 of Article 26 (Mutual Agreement Procedure) shall be deleted and replaced by the following paragraphs:

"5. Where, pursuant to a mutual agreement procedure under this Article, the competent authorities have endeavored but are unable to reach a complete agreement, the case shall be resolved through arbitration conducted in the manner prescribed by, and subject to, the requirements of paragraph 6 and any rules or procedures agreed upon by the Contracting States, if:

a) tax returns have been filed with at least one of the Contracting States with respect to the taxable years at issue in the case;

b) the case is not a particular case that both competent authorities agree, before the date on which arbitration proceedings would otherwise have begun, is not suitable for determination by arbitration; and

c) all concerned persons agree according to the provisions of subparagraph (d) of paragraph 6.

An unresolved case shall not, however, be submitted to arbitration if a decision on such case has already been rendered by a court or administrative tribunal of either Contracting State.

6. For the purposes of paragraph 5 and this paragraph, the following rules and definitions shall apply:

a) the term "concerned person" means the presenter of a case to a competent authority for consideration under this Article and all other persons, if any, whose tax liability to either Contracting State may be directly affected by a mutual agreement arising from that consideration;

b) the "commencement date" for a case is the earliest date on which the information necessary to undertake substantive consideration for a mutual agreement has been received by both competent authorities;

c) arbitration proceedings in a case shall begin on the later of:

   (i) two years after the commencement date of that case, unless both competent authorities have previously agreed to a different date, and

   (ii) the earliest date upon which the agreement required by subparagraph d) has been received by both competent authorities;

d) the concerned person(s), and their authorized representatives or agents, must agree prior to the beginning of arbitration proceedings not to disclose to any other person any information received during the course of the arbitration proceeding from either Contracting State or the arbitration panel, other than the determination of such panel;

e) unless any concerned person does not accept the determination of an arbitration panel the determination shall constitute a resolution by mutual agreement under this Article and shall be binding on both Contracting States with respect to that case only; and

f) for purposes of an arbitration proceeding under paragraph 5 and this paragraph, the members of the arbitration panel and their staffs shall be concerned "persons or authorities" to whom information may be disclosed under Article 27 (Exchange of Information) of the Convention."

ARTICLE XI

Article 27 (Exchange of Information) of the Convention shall be deleted and replaced by the following:

"Article 27

Exchange of Information

1. The competent authorities of the Contracting States shall exchange such information as may be relevant for carrying out the provisions of this Convention or to the administration or enforcement of the domestic laws concerning taxes of every kind and description imposed on behalf of the Contracting States, insofar as taxation thereunder is not contrary to the Convention. The exchange of information is not restricted by Articles 1 (Personal Scope) and 2 (Taxes Covered).

2. Any information received under this Article by a Contracting State shall be treated as secret in the same manner as information obtained under the domestic laws of that State and shall be disclosed only to persons or authorities (including courts and administrative bodies) concerned with the assessment or collection or administration of, the enforcement or prosecution in respect of, the determination of appeals in relation to the taxes referred to in paragraph 1, or the oversight of the above. Such persons or authorities shall use the information only for such purposes. They may disclose the information in public court proceedings or in judicial decisions.

3. In no case shall the provisions of paragraphs 1 and 2 be construed so as to impose on a Contracting State the obligation:

a) to carry out administrative measures at variance with the laws and administrative practice of that or of the other Contracting State;

b) to supply information which is not obtainable under the laws or in the normal course of the administration of that or of the other Contracting State;

c) to supply information which would disclose any trade, business, industrial, commercial or professional secret or trade process, or information the disclosure of which would be contrary to public policy ("ordre public").

4. a) If information is requested by a Contracting State in accordance with this Article, the other Contracting State shall use its information gathering measures to obtain the requested information, even though that other State may not need such information for its own tax purposes. The obligation contained in the preceding sentence is subject to the limitations of paragraph 3 but in no case shall such limitations be construed to permit a Contracting State to decline to supply information solely because it has no domestic interest in such information.

b) If specifically requested by the competent authority of a Contracting State, the competent authority of the other Contracting State shall, if possible, provide information under this Article in the form of depositions of witnesses and authenticated copies of unedited original documents (including books, papers, statements, records, accounts, and writings), to the same extent such depositions and documents can be obtained under the laws and administrative practices of the other Contracting State with respect to its own taxes.

c) A Contracting State shall allow representatives of the other Contracting State to enter the first-mentioned Contracting State to interview taxpayers and look at and copy their books and records, but only after obtaining the consent of those taxpayers and the competent authority of the first-mentioned State (who may be present or represented, if desired), and only if the two Contracting States agree, in an exchange of diplomatic notes, to allow such inquiries on a reciprocal basis. Such inquiries shall not be considered audits for purposes of French domestic law.

5. In no case shall the provisions of paragraph 3 be construed to permit a Contracting State to decline to supply information solely because the information is held by a bank, other financial institution, nominee or person acting in an agency or a fiduciary capacity or because it relates to ownership interests in a person."

ARTICLE XII

Paragraph 5 of Article 28 (Assistance in Collection) of the Convention shall be deleted and replaced by the following:

"The assistance provided for in this Article shall not be accorded with respect to citizens, companies, or other entities of the Contracting State to which application is made."

ARTICLE XIII

1. Paragraph 2 of Article 29 (Miscellaneous Provisions) of the Convention shall be deleted and replaced by the following:

"2. Notwithstanding any provision of the Convention except the provisions of paragraph 3, the United States may tax its residents, as determined under Article 4 (Resident) and its citizens as if the Convention had not come into effect, and France may tax entities which have their place of effective management and which are subject to tax in France as if paragraph 3 of Article 4 of the Convention had not come into effect. Notwithstanding the other provisions of this Convention, a former citizen or former long-term resident of a Contracting State may, for the period of ten years following the loss of such status, be taxed in accordance with the laws of that Contracting State, with respect to its income from, or treated as from, sources within that Contracting State. For this purpose, the term "long term resident" means, with respect to a Contracting State, any individual (other than a citizen of that Contracting State) who is a lawful permanent resident of that Contracting State in at least eight taxable years during the preceding fifteen taxable years."

2. Subparagraph b) of paragraph 3 of Article 29 (Miscellaneous Provisions) of the Convention shall be deleted and replaced by the following:

"b) the benefits conferred under paragraph 2 of Article 18 (Pensions), and under Articles 19 (Public Remuneration), 20 (Teachers and Researchers), 21 (Students and Trainees), and 31 (Diplomatic and Consular Officers), upon individuals resident in a Contracting State who are neither citizens of, nor have immigrant status in, that Contracting State."

3. In view of the amendment of Article 24 (Relief from Double Taxation) of the Convention by paragraph 1 of Article VIII of this Protocol, Subparagraph (b) of paragraph 7 of Article 29 (Miscellaneous Provisions) of the Convention, as incorporated in the alternat of the United States, in both the English and French version of such alternat, shall be deleted and replaced by the following:

"b) United States state and local income taxes on income from personal services and any other business income (except income that is exempt under subparagraph 1 a) (i) or (ii) of Article 24 (Relief from Double Taxation) shall be allowed as business expenses."

4. A new paragraph 9 of Article 29 (Miscellaneous Provisions) of the Convention shall be added as follows:

"9. Notwithstanding the provisions of Article 19 (Public Remuneration), remuneration, other than a pension, paid by France or a local authority thereof, or an agency or instrumentality of France or that authority, to an individual in respect of services rendered to France, or to that authority, agency or instrumentality shall be taxable only in the United States if the services are rendered in the United States and the individual is a resident and a national of the United States or an alien admitted to the United States for permanent residence (a "green card holder")."

ARTICLE XIV

Article 30 (Limitation on Benefits of the Convention) of the Convention shall be deleted and replaced by the following:

"Article 30

Limitation on Benefits of the Convention

1. A resident of a Contracting State shall be entitled to benefits otherwise accorded to residents of a Contracting State by this Convention only to the extent provided in this Article.

2. A resident of a Contracting State shall be entitled to all the benefits of this Convention if the resident is:

a) an individual;

b) a Contracting State, a political subdivision (in the case of the United States) or local authority thereof, or an agency or instrumentality of that State, subdivision, or authority;

c) a company, if:

(i) its principal class of shares (and any disproportionate class of shares) is regularly traded on one or more recognized stock exchanges, and either

aa) its principal class of shares is primarily traded on a recognized stock exchange located in the Contracting State of which the company is a resident (or, in the case of a company resident in France, on a recognized stock exchange located within the European Union or, in the case of a company resident in the United States, on a recognized stock exchange located in another state that is a party to the North American Free Trade Agreement); or

bb) the company's primary place of management and control is in the Contracting State of which it is a resident; or

(ii) at least 50 percent of the aggregate voting power and value of the shares (and at least 50 percent of any disproportionate class of shares) in the company are owned directly or indirectly by five or fewer companies entitled to benefits under clause (i) of this subparagraph or by persons described in subparagraph b), provided that, in the case of indirect ownership, each intermediate owner is a resident of either Contracting State;

d) a person described in clause (ii) of subparagraph (b) of paragraph 2 of Article 4 (Resident) of this Convention, provided that

(i) in the case of a pension trust and any other organization established in a State and maintained exclusively to administer or provide retirement benefits that is established or sponsored by a person that is a resident of that State under the provisions of Article 4, more than 50 percent of the person's beneficiaries, members or participants are individuals resident in either Contracting State; or

(ii) the organization sponsoring such person is entitled to the benefits of this Convention pursuant to this Article, or

e) a person other than an individual, if:

(i) on at least half the days of the taxable year at least 50 percent of the aggregate voting power and value of its shares (and at least 50 percent of any disproportionate class of shares) or other beneficial interests in the person is owned, directly or indirectly, by residents of the Contracting State of which that person is a resident that are entitled to the benefits of this Convention under subparagraph (a), subparagraph (b), clause (i) of subparagraph (c), or subparagraph (d) of this paragraph, provided that, in the case of indirect ownership, each intermediate owner is a resident of that Contracting State; and

(ii) less than 50 percent of the person's gross income for the taxable year, as determined in the person's State of residence, is paid or accrued, directly or indirectly, to persons who are not residents of either Contracting State entitled to the benefits of this Convention under subparagraph a), subparagraph b), clause (i) of subparagraph c), or subparagraph d) of this paragraph in the form of payments that are deductible for purposes of the taxes covered by this Convention in the person's State of residence (but not including arm's length payments in the ordinary course of business for services or tangible property and payments in respect of financial obligations to a bank that is not related to the payor).

f) An investment entity referred to in clause (iii) of subparagraph (b) of paragraph 2 of Article 4 (Resident) provided that more than half of the shares, rights, or interests in such entity are owned directly or indirectly by:

> (i) persons that are resident of the Contracting State of which the investment entity is a resident and that qualify for benefits under subparagraph a), subparagraph b), clause (i) of subparagraph c), or subparagraph d) of this paragraph, and

> (ii) citizens of the United States in the case of an investment entity that is a resident of the United States,

provided that, in the case of indirect ownership, each intermediate owner is a resident of the Contracting State of which the investment entity is a resident.

3. A company that is a resident of a Contracting State shall also be entitled to the benefits of the Convention if:

a) at least 95 percent of the aggregate voting power and value of its shares (and at least 50 percent of any disproportionate class of shares) is owned, directly or indirectly by seven or fewer persons that are equivalent beneficiaries; and

b) less than 50 percent of the company's gross income, as determined in the company's State of residence, for the taxable year is paid or accrued, directly or indirectly, to persons who are not equivalent beneficiaries, in the form of payments (but not including arm's length payments in the ordinary course of business for services or tangible property and payments in respect of financial obligations to a bank that is not related to the payor), that are deductible for the purposes of the taxes covered by this Convention in the company's State of residence.

4. a) A resident of a Contracting State shall be entitled to benefits of the Convention with respect to an item of income derived from the other Contracting State, regardless of whether the resident is entitled to benefits under paragraph 2 or 3 of this Article, if the resident is engaged in the active conduct of a trade or business in the first-mentioned State (other than the business of making or managing investments for the resident's own account, unless these activities are banking, insurance or securities activities carried on by a bank, insurance company or registered securities dealer), and the income derived from the other Contracting State is derived in connection with, or is incidental to, that trade or business.

b) If a resident of a Contracting State derives an item of income from a trade or business activity in the other Contracting State, or derives an item of income arising in the other Contracting State from an associated enterprise, subparagraph a) of this paragraph shall apply to such item only if the trade or business activity in the first-mentioned State is substantial in relation to the trade or business activity in the other State. Whether a trade or business activity is substantial for purposes of this paragraph shall be determined based on all the facts and circumstances.

c) In determining whether a person is "engaged in the active conduct of a trade or business" in a Contracting State under subparagraph a) of this paragraph, activities conducted by persons connected to such person shall be deemed to be conducted by such person. A person shall be connected to another person if one possesses at least 50 percent of the beneficial interest in the other (or, in the case of a company, at least 50 percent of the aggregate vote and at least 50 percent of the aggregate value of the shares in the company or of the beneficial equity interest in the company) or another person possesses, directly or indirectly, at least 50 percent of the beneficial interest (or, in the case of a company, at least 50 percent of the aggregate vote and at least 50 percent of the aggregate value of the shares in the company or of the beneficial equity interest in the company) in each person. In any case, a person shall be considered to be connected to another person if, based on all the relevant facts and circumstances, one has control of the other or both are under the control of the same person or persons.

5. Notwithstanding the preceding provisions of this Article, where an enterprise of a Contracting State derives income from the other Contracting State, and that income is attributable to a permanent establishment which that enterprise has in a third jurisdiction, the tax benefits that would otherwise apply under the other provisions of the Convention shall not apply to that income if the combined tax that is actually paid with respect to such income in the first-mentioned Contracting State and in the third jurisdiction is less than 60 percent of the tax that would have been payable in the first-mentioned State if the income were earned in that Contracting State by the enterprise and were not attributable to the permanent establishment in the third jurisdiction. Any dividends, interest or royalties to which the provisions of this paragraph apply shall be subject to tax in the other Contracting State at a rate that shall not exceed 15 percent of the gross amount thereof. Any other income to which the provisions of this paragraph apply shall be subject to tax under the provisions of the domestic law of the other Contracting State, notwithstanding any other provision of the Convention. The provisions of this paragraph shall not apply if:

a) in the case of royalties, the royalties are received as compensation for the use of, or the right to use, intangible property produced or developed by the permanent establishment itself; or

b) in the case of any other income, the income derived from the other Contracting State is derived in connection with, or is incidental to, the active conduct of a trade or business carried on by the permanent establishment in the third jurisdiction (other than the business of making, managing or simply holding investments for the enterprise's own account, unless these activities are banking or securities activities carried on by a bank or registered securities dealer).

6. A resident of a Contracting State that is not entitled to benefits pursuant to the preceding paragraphs of this Article shall, nevertheless, be granted benefits of the Convention if the competent authority of the other Contracting State determines that the establishment, acquisition or maintenance of such person and the conduct of its operations did not have as one of its principal purposes the obtaining of benefits under the Convention. The competent authority of the other Contracting State shall consult with the competent authority of the first-mentioned State before denying the benefits of the Convention under this paragraph.

7. For the purposes of this Article,

a) the term "principal class of shares" means the ordinary or common shares of the company, provided that such class of shares represents the majority of the voting power and value of the company. If no single class of ordinary or common shares represents the majority of the aggregate voting power and value of the company, the "principal class of shares" is that class or those classes that in the aggregate represent a majority of the aggregate voting power and value of the company.

b) the term "disproportionate class of shares" means any class of shares of a company resident in one of the States that entitles the shareholder to disproportionately higher participation, through dividends, redemption payments or otherwise, in the earnings generated in the other State by particular assets or activities of the company.

c) the term "shares" shall include depository receipts thereof.

d) the term "recognized stock exchange" means:

(i) the NASDAQ System owned by the National Association of Securities Dealers, Inc. and any stock exchange registered with the U.S. Securities and Exchange Commission as a national securities exchange under the U.S. Securities Exchange Act of 1934;

(ii) the French stock exchanges controlled by the "Autorité des marchés financiers";

(iii) the stock exchanges of Amsterdam, Brussels, Frankfurt, Hamburg, London, Lisbon, Madrid, Milan, Stockholm, Sydney, Tokyo, Toronto and the Swiss stock exchange; and

(iv) any other stock exchanges agreed upon by the competent authorities of the Contracting States.

e) a company's primary place of management and control shall be in the State of which it is a resident only if executive officers and senior management employees exercise day-to-day responsibility for more of the strategic, financial and operational policy decision making for the company (including its direct and indirect subsidiaries) in that State than in any other state, and the staffs conduct more of the day-to-day activities necessary for preparing and making those decisions in that State than in any other state.

f) the term "equivalent beneficiary" means a resident of a member state of the European Union or of a party to the North American Free Trade Agreement, but only if that resident:

(i)   aa) would be entitled to all the benefits of a comprehensive convention for the avoidance of double taxation between any member state of the European Union or any party to the North American Free Trade Agreement and the Contracting State from which the benefits of this Convention are claimed under provisions analogous to subparagraph a), subparagraph b), clause (i) of subparagraph c), or subparagraph d) of paragraph 2 of this Article, provided that if such convention does not contain a comprehensive limitation on benefits article, the person would be entitled to the benefits of this Convention by reason of subparagraph a), subparagraph b), clause (i) of subparagraph c), or subparagraph d) of paragraph 2 of this Article if such person were a resident of one of the Contracting States under Article 4 (Resident) of this Convention; and

bb) with respect to insurance premiums and to income referred to in Articles 10 (Dividends), 11 (Interest) or 12 (Royalties) of this Convention, would be entitled under such convention to an exemption from excise tax on such premiums or a rate of tax with respect to the particular item of income for which benefits are being claimed under this Convention that is at least as low as the rate applicable under this Convention; or

(ii) is a resident of a Contracting State that is entitled to the benefits of this Convention by reason of subparagraph a), subparagraph b), clause (i) of subparagraph c), or subparagraph d) of paragraph 2 of this Article.

For the purposes of applying paragraph 3 of Article 10 (Dividends) in order to determine whether a person owning shares, directly or indirectly, in the company claiming the benefits of this Convention is an equivalent beneficiary, such person shall be deemed to hold the same voting power in the case of a company resident of the United States, or share of the capital in the case of a company resident of France, in the company paying the dividend as the company claiming the benefits holds in such company.

g) with respect to dividends, interest, or royalties arising in France and beneficially owned by a company that is a resident of the United States, a company that is a resident of a member state of the European Union shall be treated as satisfying the requirements of subparagraph (f)(i)(bb) for purposes of determining whether such United States resident is entitled to benefits under this paragraph if a payment of dividends, interest, or royalties arising in France and paid directly to such resident of a member state of the European Union would have been exempt from tax pursuant to any directive of the European Union, notwithstanding that the income tax convention between France and that other member state of the European Union would provide for a higher rate of tax with respect to such payment than the rate of tax applicable to such United States company under Article 10 (Dividends), 11 (Interest), or 12 (Royalties) of this Convention."

ARTICLE XV

Paragraph 1 of Article 32 (Provisions for Implementation) of the Convention shall be deleted and replaced by the following:

"1. The competent authorities of the Contracting States may prescribe rules and procedures, jointly or separately, to determine the mode of application of the provisions of this Convention."

ARTICLE XVI

1. The Contracting States shall notify each other when their respective constitutional and statutory requirements for the entry into force of this Protocol have been satisfied. The Protocol shall enter into force on the date of receipt of the later of such notifications.

2. The provisions of this Protocol shall have effect:

a) in respect of taxes withheld at source, for amounts paid or credited on or after the first day of January of the year in which this Protocol enters into force;

b)   in respect of other taxes, for taxable periods beginning on or after the first day of January next following the date on which the Protocol enters into force.

3. Notwithstanding paragraph 2, the provisions of paragraphs 5 and 6 of Article 26 (Mutual Agreement Procedure) shall have effect with respect to

a) cases that are under consideration by the competent authorities as of the date on which this Protocol enters into force, and

b) cases that come under such consideration after that time,

and the commencement date for a case described in subparagraph a) of this paragraph shall be the date on which this Protocol enters into force.

IN WITNESS WHEREOF, the undersigned, being duly authorized thereto, have signed this Protocol.

DONE at Paris, in duplicate, this thirteenth day of January, 2009, in the English and French languages, each text being equally authentic.

<table>
<tr><td>**FOR THE GOVERNMENT
OF THE UNITED STATES OF
AMERICA**</td><td>**FOR THE GOVERNMENT
OF THE FRENCH REPUBLIC**</td></tr>
</table>

www.ingramcontent.com/pod-product-compliance
Lightning Source LLC
Chambersburg PA
CBHW060445290526
45793CB00002B/589